# Issun Boshi

*This story is a retelling of a traditional tale from Japan, called 'Issun-boshi'.*

by Holly Harper

illustrated by Sofia Cardoso

OXFORD
UNIVERSITY PRESS
AUSTRALIA & NEW ZEALAND

# Chapter 1
## No matter how small

An old man and an old woman lived on a farm by a river. They had no children to love and nobody to help them on the farm as they grew older. One day, the old woman decided to wish for a child.

"Please give me a son," she said. "No matter how small!"

The next day, they found a tiny baby on the doorstep.
He was no bigger than a finger. They named him Issun Boshi.

As the years went by, Issun Boshi got older, but he never
grew any taller. Issun Boshi didn't mind though, because he
was very clever.

Issun Boshi helped his parents on the farm every day. It wasn't very exciting. He wanted to go to the city where he could have an adventure.

He begged his mother and father to let him go, and when he was old enough they agreed.

They knew it was a long way to the city, so they gave him a needle for a walking stick.

"Goodbye, Issun Boshi!" his mother and father said. "Have fun on your adventure!"

They were going to miss Issun Boshi, but they knew he was clever enough to get himself out of any trouble ... no matter how big!

## Chapter 2
## The long journey

Issun Boshi set out along the road to the city. He had never been so far from home, and he was excited to see the city.

It was a long journey. He walked and walked. Even after a whole day, he still hadn't gone far because he was so small.

"There has to be a smarter way," he said.

He called out to a man on a cart to give him a ride, but the man couldn't hear him.

Issun Boshi's feet began to ache, so he decided to dip them in the river. He discovered an old rice bowl and a chopstick in the reeds.

"Somebody must have thrown them away," he said. "If I use this rice bowl as a boat, I'll arrive in the city in no time!"

He dragged the bowl into the river and used the chopstick to help him steer it. The rice bowl sailed down the rushing river.

Soon, Issun Boshi was close to the city.

When he reached the city, Issun Boshi climbed out of his boat and started to explore. The streets of the city were so full that Issun Boshi was nearly stepped on many times. Thinking quickly, he grabbed onto the sandal of a man walking past.

The man didn't see Issun Boshi. The tiny boy held on tight as the man walked up the street and in his front gate. When the man took off his sandals, Issun Boshi climbed up.

He looked around and was amazed. He had never seen a house so big in his life! It wasn't a house, it was a castle. The man who lived here must be important. Issun Boshi went inside to say hello but, before he could find the man, he heard a girl wail.

# Chapter 3

## The princess

"Where is it?" asked the girl. She looked like a princess.

"Where's my golden hairpin? I can't find it anywhere!
I'm going to be in trouble if I can't find it."

Issun Boshi spotted something gleaming on the ground.

"Is this it?" he asked.

The princess gasped. "Who are you?"

"I'm Issun Boshi," he said.

"Who are you talking to, my daughter?" asked the man.

"It's a tiny person," said the princess. "His name is Issun Boshi."

The man gasped, too. "How did you get past the guards?"

"I held onto your sandal so that I wouldn't get crushed!" said Issun Boshi.

"What a clever thing to do!" said the princess.

The man could see that the princess liked Issun Boshi, and he did, too.

"Would you like to come and work for me?" he asked.

Issun Boshi thought that working for an important man in a castle could be a wonderful adventure.

"Yes please!" he said, and bowed.

Issun Boshi liked working in the castle. Even though he was small, he still found ways to help because he was so clever.

Everybody in the castle liked Issun Boshi, but the princess liked him most of all. She was clever, too, and they soon became best friends.

# Chapter 4
## The hungry troll

One day, the princess decided to go for a walk. Issun Boshi went with her to keep her company. As they walked along the river, they heard a shout.

"Help me," said a man. "I was on my way to the market to sell my fruit when something pounced on my cart!"

"It's a troll," said the princess. "He looks hungry!"

"Maybe he'll stop if we ask him to," said Issun Boshi.

"Watch out!" said the princess. "Trolls can be dangerous."

"Hello there," said Issun Boshi.

The troll just kept eating.

Issun Boshi started to climb up on the cart so the troll could hear him, but he slipped and fell into the pile of fruit. The troll reached down and scooped up a handful of fruit. He popped it all in his mouth – Issun Boshi included!

# Chapter 5
# Big trouble

Issun Boshi fell into the troll's mouth. He knew he was in big trouble. If he didn't do something quickly, he would be swallowed. He thought quickly, and then he had an idea.

Issun Boshi reached for his needle and began to tickle the troll's tongue.

The troll was very ticklish. He began to chuckle, then he let out a big laugh. As soon as the troll's mouth was open, Issun Boshi jumped out.

Luckily the princess was there to catch him. The troll was so surprised to see a tiny boy jump out of his mouth that he gave a yelp of fright and ran away.

"Issun Boshi, that was really clever!" said the princess.
"I was worried that you were in big trouble."

"I was worried, too," said Issun Boshi.

The fruit seller thanked Issun Boshi and the princess,
then he pulled his cart away. The princess noticed something
lying in the road.

"Hey, look at that," she said. "Is that what I think it is?"

# Chapter 6

## The wish

"What is it?" asked Issun Boshi.

"It's the troll's mallet," said the princess. "He left it behind. It's not just a normal mallet, it's a wish mallet!" She turned to Issun Boshi. "You can use it to wish for anything!"

Issun Boshi thought about it. "Could I wish to be big?" he asked.

"You could," said the princess, "but why do you want to be big? You're already smarter than somebody ten times bigger than you."

Issun Boshi frowned. "What if we see another troll? Nearly being swallowed wasn't very pleasant. I don't want it to happen again."

"That's another clever thought," said the princess.

Issun Boshi touched the mallet's handle and wished ...

Suddenly, the mallet vanished.

Issun Boshi began to grow and grow. Soon he was just as tall as the princess ... even a little bit taller!

"Now you're the small one," he told her.

The princess laughed. "Come on, let's go back to the castle!" she said.

Issun Boshi and the princess stayed friends for life, and nobody ever swallowed Issun Boshi again.